DOGS SET III

Shih Tzus

Bob Temple

ABDO Publishing Company

visit us at
www.abdopub.com

Published by ABDO Publishing Company, 4940 Viking Drive, Suite 622, Edina, Minnesota 55435.

Printed in the United States

Edited by: Paul Joseph

Photo credits: Peter Arnold, Inc.; Ron Kimball Photography

Library of Congress Cataloging-in-Publication Data

Temple, Bob.
     Shih tzus / Bob Temple
          p. cm. — (Dogs. Set III)
     ISBN 1-57765-423-4
     1. Shih tzu—Juvenile literature. [1. Shih tzu. 2. Dogs. 3. Pets] I. Title.

SF429.S64 T46 2000
636.76—dc21
                    00-036180

Contents

Where Dogs Come From

Humans have found joy and friendship in dogs for thousands of years. There are millions of dogs that are family pets in the world today. Some dogs do more than just act as **companions.** Some dogs also work with their human owners, herding sheep or helping out on a hunting trip, for example.

Thousands of years ago, some breeds of dog were adopted by kings and queens and became symbols for an entire country. The Shih Tzu is one such dog.

All dogs are from the species called Canidae, from the Latin word canis, which means "dog." This is why you sometimes hear dogs called "canines." Some members of this family of animals still live in the wild. Wolves and foxes are members of this family.

Shih Tzus

Shih Tzus are from the "toy" group of dogs. This is because they are very small. Shih Tzus are known for their silky hair that grows long all over their bodies, even on their faces. Because of this, most Shih Tzu owners put their dog's hair in a topknot. Sometimes, they even use a beautiful bow.

"Shih Tzu" is a Chinese word that means "lion" or "lion dog." They first became popular dogs in China in the seventh century. They became a favorite dog of Chinese royalty, and many sculptures and paintings in China include a Shih Tzu. They were brought to England in the 1930s and came to America along with soldiers returning from World War II.

Opposite page: Shih Tzus have long, silky hair.

What They're Like

Shih Tzus make great family pets. They love to play with people and to have their long **coats** brushed. They are very good with children, so long as they don't get too rough. Because they are very small, it's easy to hurt a Shih Tzu with rough play. Shih Tzus love to be outside and play in all kinds of weather. They are very quick, and should always be kept on a leash when they are outside.

Shih Tzus are very happy little dogs that love to be in the middle of a busy family. They must live indoors with the family, but they love to go on walks with their owners. Even though they are small, they make good watchdogs. They have a lot of courage, and they will bark when they are surprised.

Opposite page: The Shih Tzu is a great family pet.

Coat and Color

Its beautiful **coat** is a big part of what makes a Shih Tzu special. It is very thick, long, and flowing. Some Shih Tzus might have wavy hair, but not curly. Even the hair on top of their noses grows long. The topknots that many owners put on their Shih Tzus heads help keep the fur out of the dog's eyes.

Shih Tzus can be any color, from white to black. Most Shih Tzus have more than one color in their fur.

Opposite page: Most Shih Tzus fur is a mixture of black and white.

Size

Shih Tzus are very small dogs, but they are not among the smallest dogs in the toy group. They usually weigh between nine and 18 pounds (4.1 to 8.2 kg). They stand 9 to 10 inches tall (22.9 to 26.7 cm).

They have a round head with a square, short muzzle that makes it appear like they have a pushed-in face. Their eyes are dark and round. Their ears are long and hang down at the sides.

Opposite page: The Shih Tzu is a very small dog.

Care

At first glance, most people are impressed at how beautiful the Shih Tzu's **coat** looks. Shih Tzu owners must be prepared to work very hard to make their dogs look like that, especially if they are going to become show dogs. To keep that coat from getting matted, it should be brushed every day.

When you give your Shih Tzu a bath, you will need to blow dry its hair, too. Keeping your dog's head hair up in a ribbon or barrette will help keep his eyes healthy, too. If you don't want to bathe your dog often, a trim will keep the hair from dragging on the ground when it is outside.

Your dog's eyes should be checked every day. His teeth and ears need to be checked and cleaned at least once a week.

Shih Tzus don't need as much exercise as larger dogs, but they do need to be taken on walks. A good game of fetch, indoors or out, will also help keep your dog healthy. Because of their pushed-in nose, Shih Tzus sometimes have breathing problems, so they should be kept out of very hot or very cold weather.

All dogs need shots every year to keep them from getting diseases like **distemper** and **rabies.** Another thing that will keep your Shih Tzu happy and healthy is giving him a lot of love and attention.

A Shih Tzu should be brushed every day.

Feeding

It is important to make sure that your dog gets the right kind of food. Getting the right **nutrition** will help keep your Shih Tzu happy, healthy, and looking pretty.

When you first bring your puppy home, you should continue to feed it the same food that the breeder was using. This will keep your puppy from getting an upset stomach.

Puppies are usually fed twice each day, and as they get older, they often need just one feeding. If you want to change your dog's diet, you should do it slowly. Check with your **veterinarian** to find the food that is right for your dog. Always make sure your Shih Tzu has plenty of clean, fresh water to drink, too.

Opposite page: Shih Tzus need a proper diet to stay healthy.

Things They Need

One thing your Shih Tzu is going to need more than anything else is attention. Shih Tzus love to be brushed, petted, and pampered. They also love to be played with. But your Shih Tzu is also going to need a quiet, warm place to sleep. If you don't provide one for him, you might find that he wants to sleep in your bed with you.

Shih Tzus need to live indoors, not outside in a kennel. They also love to be outside. When your Shih Tzu is outside, it should be on a leash with you, not tied up to a chain and left alone.

To keep your dog safe, you should make sure that she has a collar with a tag that includes your name, address, and telephone number. That way, if your dog gets lost, the person who finds her can contact you. In many cities, dogs also need to have a **license**. Many dogs also wear a tag that says they have gotten their **rabies** shot.

In order to be a good member of the family, your Shih Tzu also needs to be trained. Basic commands like sit, stay, and down can make your dog a better member of the family and help keep it safe, too.

Shih Tzus need a warm, quiet place to rest.

Puppies

Shih Tzus have two to four puppies in a **litter**. The puppies' **coats** usually change color after they are born. After about 18 months to two years, your Shih Tzu will be full-grown. If they are healthy, they usually live 10 to 12 years.

All dogs are **mammals,** which means they drink milk from their mother's body when they are first born. After four or five weeks, you can begin to feed them soft puppy food.

Puppies need many different shots in order for them to stay healthy. If you bring home a Shih Tzu puppy, you should take it to the **veterinarian** as soon as possible to get its life with you started in the right direction.

Opposite page: Shih Tzus are usually full grown by two years old.

Glossary

coat: the hair that covers a dog's body.

companion: one that keeps company with another; a friend.

distemper: a contagious disease that dogs sometimes get. It is caused by a virus.

license (LIE-sense): a tag worn by a dog indicating it has been registered with a city.

litter: the group of puppies a dog has in one pregnancy.

mammal: warm-blooded animals that feed their babies milk from the mother's body.

nutrition (new-TRISH-un): food; nourishment.

rabies: a serious virus that is very dangerous to dogs.

veterinarian (VET-er-in-AIR-ian): your dog's doctor; also called a vet.

Internet Sites

The American Shih Tzu Club
http://www.shihtzu.org
The Official Web site of the Shih Tzu. Learn about health concerns, the history of the breed, how to care for your Shih Tzu, where to find a breeder, and much more.

American Kennel Club of America
http://www.akc.org
Find tips for buying a Shih Tzu puppy, including breeder references, and information about the club at this site. Read the American Kennel Club's standard for the breed, find out about health problems common to Shih Tzus, and find regional clubs to join, too.

Index